SWERVE

SWERVE

poems on

environmentalism

feminism

and

resistance

Ellery Akers

blue light press * 1st world publishing

san francisco * fairfield * delhi

Blue Light Press
www.bluelightpress.com
bluelightpress@aol.com

1st World Publishing
PO Box 2211
Fairfield, IA 52556
www.1stworldpublishing.com

First Edition
ISBN: 978-1-421836-40-9

Library of Congress Control Number: 2019950328

ALSO BY ELLERY AKERS

poetry

Practicing the Truth
Knocking on the Earth

children's books

Sarah's Waterfall

For Rachel Carson

Contents

3. RESISTANCE

SWERVE

1. THE EARTH

Lesions

"Starfish have been dying by the millions . . . along the U.S. West Coast . . ."

—*Daily Mail* Online

Whenever a species gets stubbed out like this,
I feel the border of our lives is fraying:
the map of the sea yanked blank in one corner.
Sometimes I think we're holding the diameter
of the earth in our hands—
an elastic band, stretched tight—
and we're living in the years
before it snaps back
and tosses animals and trees and us away.
Maybe we should write a letter to those people of the future:
Here is the earth. Love it for us.
It's hard to believe, but we loved it, too.

Our Grief for the Earth Is Hidden

1. The Diminished World

Most of the time I don't want to know about it

But whatever we can't understand is falling as rain into moraines
    and vernal pools
hissing onto the soaked canopies of alders with their leaf scars
so the branches are shaking
and the seas are rising

When I was born I thought I'd be taken from the earth
I didn't think the earth would be taken from me

2. Fewer

The monarchs
are fewer

just one or two today fluttering over the ocean

Sometimes I can't stand to think of the sea becoming barren
the kelp gone   the sculpin

just a sheen on the water

At least we can't thin the stars out of the sky

3. Journey of an Environmentalist

After I'd locked myself in with my petitions
and my checkbook and my computer,
and after I'd given up reading the news,
because reading the news was like opening a freezer
and smelling stale ice—
I sat down next to the grass
and fell in love with the earth again:
I noticed the grass blades
had hairs that looked the same
as the hairs on the back of my hand—
blade meet hand, meet blade.

4. To the Insects Who Are Leaving Us

You never seemed to steer. You mostly fluttered or wavered
or sank a little in the air.
Once in while you aimed—at an intruder, at a hive.
Once in a while you dropped.
Once in a while you drifted onto a page I was reading
and I blew you gently away.
Lacewings. Thrips.

Once I saw a lake surrounded by banks of forget-me-nots—
they lifted and floated away—*damselflies!*

Boxelder bugs stuck end to end in spring,
mating and walking along at the same time—
Crickets with ears in their knees—
Dragonflies eating mosquitoes,
discarding their wings in a glittering pile—

If you love insects you can never feel alone, said one entomologist.

There is Roundup in the air and in the rain.
Atrazine in the snow. Neonics in the honey.

Sometimes I stopped to watch you shine:

With your chitin. With your stingers. With your pollen.

After the Inauguration

I go out and apologize to the leaves.
I'm sorry, I say. I love the way you shake in the wind.
The way you uncrinkle in the spring
so that each of you
gets a chance at the light.

April 14, 2017: Reading the News

"Donald Trump's EPA Chief Scott Pruitt Calls for an Exit from the Paris Climate Agreement"

—*The Sydney Morning Herald*

This morning I see that 100 men in suits are willing to throw away the world so they can have more green rectangles made from trees.

It's spring. Plum blossoms speckle the sidewalk and fall onto my shoes, flake after flake.

I keep reminding myself I don't know how it's going to end. Attila scorched and divided, but the grass from those burnt blades grew over him.

The Buddhist Practice of Bowing

". . . I bow with all beings to attain liberation."
—Katagiri Roshi

I bow to iron bracelets as they clank on the arms of prisoners,
to shackles, handcuffs,
to the charm bracelets that jangled on my mother's arms,
to the daisy chains I made as a child—
the broken green stems smelled juicy,
the way the grass smells after a rain.

I bow to the woman who bought a thousand-dollar Coach bag,
and also to the woman
who bought a gallon of milk at the Dollar Store.

It's almost impossible to bow to the Koch brothers,
so instead I bow to the electrons of longing
zinging around inside them.

I bow to the young men
who love cars,
who love speed, chrome, gasoline,
who batter themselves against the mistake
as the mistake batters them.

Even our money
is longing
for the forest it came from.

Brainwire: Government Men

Brainwire has no use for the body. Brainwire thinks soil is for leaching. Rocks for scorching. Brainwire talks about *the cloud*. Is in a hurry. I'm in a hurry, too; we're all in a hurry. Brainwire, will you stop poking me with your electrical prong? I just want to stand here, breathed on by trees.

Reasons to Love the Sea

Because it has no core.
Because sometimes it's all dark cramp and sargasso.
Because it's stingray and swordfish and blades.
Because sea lions sigh in the dark and water sprinkles at the end
    of their whiskers.
Because a cormorant dives and brings up a herring in his bill
    and shakes it and shakes it.
Because it reflects the pale bellies of boats.
Because shearwaters cross back and forth across it,
    forty thousand miles a year.
Because lobsters march in formation at the bottom.
Because the dead rain to the bottom.
Because when a gull shits on the sea, it looks like a stream of chalk.
Because it's heartless and cold and alive and it stinks.
Because at noon it looks like light on a platter.
Because it's a great discarder,
and spits out crates and slats, and gallon jugs, and tar.
Because we sail across it in our stiff ships
and try to forget that wherever we are
everything underneath is loosening and sliding.
Because of spray. Scud. Clumps of foam that skid along the beach,
By-the-Wind Sailors that glint like cellophane.
Because rivers unravel and lose their cold in its volume;
gulls blink like sparks in the sweep of a lighthouse beam.
Because of its lacquer on a calm night, distinct.
Because when I'm swimming
I can see the small starved lights on the shore.

What I Know

How to hold a kinglet in my hand
so I don't break its wings and it doesn't bite my thumb,
how it lies in my palm, stunned,
until it starts up and bolts into the air

I know the mustards—the Cruciferae—
some of the snapdragons, some of the vetch—

On the Farallones, I know the cliffs: the calls:
the shrieking in the air

I know the murmur from a thousand murre throats
as a peregrine flies over the colony, and one by one
they take off, frightened, then dozens, hundreds,
and sprinkle into the sea

I know the sound of a humpback slapping the water with his fin,
his breath stinking of krill,
the sound of his spout like a steam engine hissing

I've seen the way spray lifts over Arch Rock and runnels down
and soaks all the sleeping sea lions so their pelts turn dark

I've seen fish veering at the same time, mackerel, sardines

I know which tracks are skink tracks in the forest
I know how to find the star zigadene every spring

I know the history of this snag: I was here when an owl landed
and a branch broke and the owl flapped away

I know the names of the machines that cut down the forest
feller buncher, shovel logger, tower yarder, stroke delimber, skidder

I don't know how to *safeguard, stand in front of, shelter*
except to speak
as if a word could *shelter*
but I don't know what word that would be

Freeway

Pigeons clatter up from an underpass. A mullein grows next to a drain, remembering the smell of the river that used to be here. Clumps of cattle hair stuck on barbed wire—gone—a tree frog that blurts from a ditch—gone. The same house repeats itself. Trees flash past. Horses. Steel exit signs, made by prisoners we never see.

Thinking About Water

How it tastes different in a Dixie cup or a china mug
How I stand with my thumb over a hose
and spritz it onto the roses
and listen as it spills across their leaves
How it is underneath us and above us, in our blood and eyes
and pipes in the walls but we forget it is not ours
How water striders and backswimmers skid over it
How we know it by its sounds as it sluices or crashes or slips away
How it waits obediently at the faucet
How it can be poisoned but never cut in two with a knife
How it is broken into over and over
by the talons of osprey
pushed aside by the webs of mallards
but still it closes again
I love the way it smells different on a lawn, a sidewalk
in a marsh, a river, a lake
I love the way it never argues or makes a point
as the wind makes a point
but always lets go and slides away

Living in the Country During the Iraq War

Every night now, I lie on cool sheets
and think of the burning. The sound of feet running
on gravel, the sound of fire louder than water.
I try not to look at the headlines
as I move from room to room in clean clothes
drinking a glass of ice water.
It's quiet here, but I feel uneasy.
Under the silence: the fire.
I drop a letter in a mailbox,
the lid closes with a clank
and under the clank
is the sound of the fire.
Women running on gravel in sandals.
I'm uneasy taking a bath. Gardening.
Walking under the deep shade of Douglas fir.
It's there under everything: the sound of the fire.
Women in sandals, running.

Buying Up the Grass

It started with the snap of a branch,
a fence, a corral,
the word *mine*,
the small factories of chlorophyll
we think work for us.

A Short History of the Sea

In the beginning it rained for centuries—
years of water pouring from one sodden cloud
onto the scooped-out hole in the earth
left by the moon, after it shot out and floated into the sky.
It was overcast for hundreds of years:
there was nothing but blank water and rock.

Finally a cell stuck to a cell
until there were seaweeds
and animals that climbed onto rock
and plants with roots
and trees and Pontiacs and dimes
and groceries and senators and strychnine.

Every year now I notice what washes onto shore—
not just bones, or wings with their feathers missing,
or whiskers of seals,
but dead seals, hypodermics,
headless plastic dolls from Japan,

bottles from the raft of plastic in the ocean,
some still rubbing against each other in the water,
the way beluga whales squeak as they dive deeper and deeper
to find food in the Arctic
and whistle to each other,
and rub up against each other, and moan.

Costco

It's an ice cavern, with miles of shelves.
We feel small and alone in the aisles:
crates of TVs, refrigerators.
The cashier's bored, the ceiling's too high.
It's getting colder;
stalactites drill into the floor.
A man encased in ice is using a forklift
to bring down a box of dinosaur bones,
tusks of mammoths,
and the blunt clubs we used to kill them with,
cold and cheap at the price.

What Nature Teaches Us

That it slows you down
so you can hear the stream as it pours

It reminds you
you are in the body it made for you

The quiet in the deep ground reminds you
The rock gouged by wind

You can stand under a tree
as it rests in its own frank love of itself—

Rarely you see this in a man or woman,
often in a tree—

In the glare and heat you can hear a garter snake slide across gravel

Your body likes to sit and watch the day moon

and you're surrounded by chlorophyll
as it binds the sun in the leaves

and you sit under those leaves

in the calm air

and your mind surrenders its locomotives

and you breathe

The Environmentalist Talks to Herself

1. *Loving the Land*

With its sloughs; with its ferns—sword, chain, goldback,
bracken—with its smell of grass blades caught in a lawnmower;
with its smell of stone, which has many smells—dry; stung with
sun; covered in clubmoss; drenched in rivers; drenched in rain;
with its smell of gravel after a rain; with its hawks, hunched and
sullen, perched on telephone lines after a rain.

2. *Loving the Sea*

Because of its shine, because of its fog, because of dried seaweed
stuck to a plank—because of slipper shells, mussel shells, because
of the sound of sea lions slapping the water, exhaling loud hoarse
breaths as they float up the coast.

3. *Calling Its Names*

Conch; Coarse Fern Spores; Egret That Kicks Her Legs in Front
of Her to Scare up Fish; Monarchs Folding and Unfolding Their
Wings on Coyote Scat; Stump; Samara;

Whose names are on my skin, whose names I call whenever I'm
alone and who answer: Foxfire, Deliverer.

4. *Negotiating with Despair*

Because I remember Rachel Carson: her shyness and caring.
Because madness is fast and sanity is slow.
She called the facts to her.
They turned into ink. Into words.

She would say:
I know how much you love
this packed, splintered, fragrant world.

You have stood. You have listened. Be patient.
You would not have been given this assignment
if you were not strong enough to hold the news in your bones.

2. THE WOMEN

#MeToo: Women in Touch with Their Anger

In one of Grimm's Fairy Tales, *the good girl goes to a pool and
a troll appears in the water and asks to be combed; she complies,
and as a reward, gold coins fall out of her mouth. The bad girl
refuses, and as a penalty, toads fall out of her mouth.*

She comes to the pool, where the head floats up
and wants to be combed.
"Comb me," he says,
but she is the bad girl this time:
"Comb yourself," she says,
and cracks the pitcher over his head:
bits of snail shell, marsh-muck, silt.

And will she go home and find, as a punishment,
fish gasping in her bed,
or will she have to run into the woods
sent out in her shoes of paper
to find strawberries in the snow?
Or will it be toads this time,
whenever she opens her mouth?
It is toads.

But think of that good girl and her fate,
the clatter of metal every time she speaks.
On her wedding night, coins clink on her pillow,
the gold falls into her arms
and wakes her: it's cold.

Her husband follows her from room to room,
ready to catch what falls—small talk, love talk.

In the alleys, on the cobbles,
people introduce themselves.
It would be impolite to refuse;
she shakes hands, says her name.
They wait for her to leave;
they stoop, they open their purses.

No, better to be the other one, the dark-haired one,
toads falling out of her mouth,
but at least this time she is not alone;
she has come to love them, the ugly toads, the venomous toads,
the ones she has been hiding:
they comfort her, they sing, they are alive.

Women and Nature

1. Barbara McClintock, geneticist

She spends her life with corn.
Every day she lifts another strand of silk.
"I start with the seedling
and I don't want to leave it.
I don't feel I really know the story
if I don't watch the plant
all the way along.
So I know every plant in the field."

2. Suzanne Simard, forest ecologist

She walks through the forest
and knows what's under her shoes:
fir and birch sending messages to each other
through their roots.
"A forest is a cooperative system, " she says,
". . . trees talk."

3. Jane Goodall, primatologist

She wears the same clothes in the forest for years
so she won't scare the chimpanzees.
"I stood, as darkness fell," she says,
"with one hand on the still warm trunk of a tree
and looked at the sparkling of an early moon . . ."

4. Wangari Maathai, environmental activist

She never forgets the stream she drank from as a child.
Her husband calls her "too strong-minded for a woman."
In divorce court she scolds the judge:
he sends her to jail.
When she gets out of jail
she and her group
plant 51 million trees.
". . . you can't do it alone," she says.

Smoke

War is one group of people
who are going to die

making sure another group of people
who are going to die

die sooner.

And so, rubble, shrapnel,
a girl in a torn skirt
face down in a ditch.

She was going to die anyway,
but this way she died sooner.

The Encounter at Twenty: New York City

The day that it happened,
my teacher had written *crap* on the bottom of my first poem:
I wanted to throw it into the Hudson
where it would sink with its *no*
under the gulls, under the garbage scows, and the litter.
What I had written was flawed, but it was mine,
and as I walked down the stairs,
into the station, past an Orange Julius counter—
juice sloshing in a vat—I noticed a poster:
At 31, Gauguin just got out
so I started to think how *I* could get out
and I decided to ride to the botanical gardens.
I walked to the back of the park
and sat under a tree.
I wasn't thinking of the chance I was taking—
I just wanted to stitch myself together with a few blades of grass—
when a man uncrumpled himself from somewhere
and stood and said, "Talk to me."
I got up and he followed
and as I thought, *Don't run yet,* I started to run,
he started to run, he tore off my coat and threw it down,
we wrestled back and forth on that asphalt path,
I couldn't think, I was flailing,
when a businessman—
briefcase in one hand, folded *New York Times* in the other—
saw us and stopped and backed away:
the guy let go of my dress, bolted,
I ran for the guard

and I stood that night in the subway car
and stared at the scuffed windows
where someone had spelled out *slut, cunt*
in the dust with his thumb.

The Woman Who Healed Herself

She became a forest floor: pine needles, chips of bark.
She became a sink full of hair, a floor full of sweepings.
She became two bandages, side by side.
She became a walker at night, night air a collar
around her throat,
and she wore the stars, too,
when she was able.
She became a shout in the night.
A mother to herself.
Two sticks rubbing together.
Timpani.
She became her own mast, her own sail.
Years she would sail: the smell of caulk and tar.
Zero would float out of her mouth and drift away.

Night Thoughts

In the dream
women climb the mountain,
but they climb it from inside, in the dark.

After the Rape: The Vow

She swore No over and over and Never
with its grey sheen
until it became a river that divided her.

And after she had taken the vow,
set a clock by the vow,
to ring No the alarm

and after she had broken the back of her sexuality
and after she had sealed her mouth both with honey and with bees
and after she had replaced love with endeavor

and after she had spent years visiting in a small room
talking to a woman
a door shut tight for privacy

and after she had spent 3,000 nights in bed with the vow beside her
and after she had tried to dismantle the vow
with its sheetrock and timber

she said, God keep us from what we swear,
we have to carry it
all our lives.

The Sibyl Speaks of the Fire

". . . only the wounded physician can heal."
—C. J. Groesbeck, *C.G. Jung and the Shaman's Vision*

First I was on fire, standing in a river.
Then I was just on fire.
The blaze made me tired:
the polish of flames, even at night.
No one told me this, but I will tell you:
I stood in the fire to become a guide to the fire.
So that when another woman stood there,
I had a map to the ash. I had a charter.
I could tell her: *One day your sleeves will cool.*
Your life will not smolder forever.

Dandelion Woman

says the earth will not be scorched beyond repair.
Her name means "tooth of the lion."
She knows how to make aspirin out of willow bark.
The rain likes her, the grass likes her,
she says *no* to hotels with gold doorknobs, *no* to *Vogue*.
She's not defined by the stares of men:
she's defined by the gaze of stars.
She knows what's outside her is inside her:
the calcium in her bones from shells,
the iron in her blood
from crusts on rocks
that leached into the sea.
She knows nothing is divided:
the wind parts the grass
the same way she parts her hair.
She has enough when she smells the forest.
She loves minerals, she loves stones:
she leans on basalt and chert as if they were sofas.
She knows how to shake this old furnace of a world
until it coughs up what's choking its core.

3. RESISTANCE

At Any Moment, There Could Be a Swerve in a Different Direction

There was a moment
when shooting egrets for feathers became wrong.
There was a moment
when the Wilderness Act
changed the lives of billions of blades of grass.

I remember the moment when a river that used to catch fire
turned from flammable to swimmable.

A swerve smells astringent, like the wind off the sea;
it tastes red, the way Red Hot cinnamon mints
burn in your mouth;
it's heavy, the way the weight of letters is heavy,
arriving in sacks at the Senate;
it sounds like the click of needles
as hundreds of thousands of women knit pink hats;
it looks like a coyote, crossing the freeway to go home.

Rachel Carson

I think of the way she bent over tide pools at night:
a woman stooped in the dark with her flashlight
as if she were stepping into the lit harness of her work.

I think of the way she lay under the stars
because they were medicine:

Tumors near the collarbone.
Pain in her spine.
Radiation. Krebiozen.
Arthritis. Iritis.
Sightless for weeks.
Listening as her friend read a draft out loud.

Remembering the robin that fell dead from a branch.

I think of the pages of notes about pesticides—

I moan inside—and I wake in the night and cry out silently
    for Maine—

And then, more notes about pesticides.

I think of the way the moon glazed the water
when she crossed out words and wrote other words.

I think of the way she knew that eels slid from brook to brook
and then to the sea.

I'm in luck,
because brown is cheapest, she said,
when she bought a wig
to cover her bald head at the Senate.

I could never again
listen happily to a thrush song, she said,
if I had not done
all I could.

They called her *spinster.*
Alarmist.
Communist.

I think of the eagles who came back because of her.
I think of her open gaze. Her resolve.
Her refusal to turn away from the wreck.

Not Too Late

The blackberry leaves that turn silver
when they flip over in the wind
know there is still time.
The charred trunks are still alive under the scorched bark.
The corals have not been completely bleached;
newts still float languidly in the pond,
and beetles, who have always carried the sun on their backs,
carry the minutes;
the mites are lugging the seconds
over the cold grains of soil;
grasshoppers move toward us with their ears on their bellies,
as if they were listening to the future;
the cardinals are fluttering,
the egrets are strutting toward us in their elegant way:
they are bringing us platters of time
and laying them down in front of us,
the hawks carrying hours in their talons
and letting them fall,
the ocean, with its clumps of foam,
delivering the weeks and months,
and even the snakes
curling around the strength of the time that's left.

Taking Action

> *"We live in capitalism. Its power seems inescapable. So did the divine right of kings. Any human power can be resisted and changed by human beings."*
>
> —Ursula K. Le Guin

It's good to act. To lean into the body of the world.
To know lawyers sit at airports with signs
saying *We Can Help* written in Farsi.

It's good to stop machines—giant needles that drill into the earth—
because what they are stitching is *The End.*

To see soldiers who wear camouflage—
shirts and pants that look like leaves and bark—
kneel in front of the Sioux
and say they're sorry for what's been taken,
even the language for *leaves* and *bark.*

It's good to signal to the others who are shocked,
to know we're not alone in shock,
that when we drive past a house
we know someone is sitting in a chair in front of a TV, shocked.

But the men who want to make us afraid
are afraid.

And my time on earth
is a huge breath:

I can blow that breath into the world.

We Have the Power to Pull Back from the Brink

*"The most common way people give up their power
is by thinking they don't have any."*

—Alice Walker

And so I stand here and call power.
I stand here and call water.

I call creeks. Lakes.
Pools. Sinkholes.
Tide pools with turban snails
and starfish—the ones
that have come back to the West Coast,
climbing over rocks on white tube feet,
resilient, as nature can be resilient.

I call shinbones of water skinnying down into sluice boxes.
Brackish water, sulfur-smelling water, sludge.
Rain in rain barrels,
clear water spilling over dams
and clear water that has never been dammed.

I confront the brink
even though I'm part of the brink.

I call snow geese sifting onto the rice fields, honking.
White-fronted geese. Brant.

I call the shapes of leaves: spatulate, cordate, pinnate, lanceolate.

I call the hole in the ozone.
Pollen. Luciferin. Chitin.

I call rare plants and animals coming back because of the fire:
fishers, black-backed woodpeckers, globe mallows, morels.

I call fire.

And fire answers
with its flaming mouth and strange whining pronunciation
as it clears the underbrush

and the hole in the ozone answers that it is closing

and the leaves answer *a twelve-year-old boy planted a million trees*

And luciferin blinks on and off
and illuminates what has been buried so long
under tons of dark water

and pollen blows into the faces of climbers
who hung all night in slings from the St. John's Bridge
to stop Shell drilling the Arctic

and water answers
Belize banned offshore oil
and protected the second largest barrier reef in the ocean

and my power answers
I've always known my hand could have been a leaf.
Hemoglobin and chlorophyll almost the same.
Only one atom different.

Why There Is Reason to Hope

For Katy Miller Johnson and all the environmentalists who saved Point Reyes National Seashore from development

Because many people love the delicate ferns.

Because many people love streams.

It's not all brackish. It's not all Clorox.

Trees grow out of the slash of the burn.

Clouds inside us travel up and down our spines.

I've seen teenagers willing to be handcuffed outside of Congress.
I've seen a girl in a raincoat
protesting in front of the Swedish Parliament.

I've seen grown men crawl over gravel
so as not to disturb cormorants at their nests.

And when I walk this trail

I remember the condominiums that were going to be built here;
I remember the blueprints with their windows and doors;

I remember the people who loved salmonberry, huckleberry:

they are the ones who said *stop*. Who said *no*.

21 Kids Sue the Government for Not Protecting Them from Climate Change

Trump tries to derail Our Children's Trust lawsuit

We can do this.
We can thread a needle with a river and stitch up the drought.
We can spill cash out of drawers—all those Presidents,
Washington, Jefferson—
lying face down in cool steel
and put them to work
to pay for lawyers for the kids
who see their future grated into powder.
We can take the fleece of the clouds
and the fleece of the sheep
and the fleece of the scud of foam on the beach
and throw it across the lies
of the men
who want to fleece us.
The ones who want to lie down in money
and pull its green quilt over their heads
the way apes twist off leaves
to make beds in the forest.
We can do this.
We can remember everything around us—
even the most alien—polystyrene, polypropylene—
has been dug from the ground.
We can leave the beautiful dark carbon
to ferment in its slots in the ground.
We don't need to poke out the last of the Permian;
we can love the vault below us and above us,

the sparkles in its rim and its design.
Because the coal in the heart of the President
who loves coal is a dead coal.
We can take this damage and make boats out of it.
We can make windmills.
We can grow runner beans.
We can take this damage and make orchards.
We can take this damage and make forests.
We can grieve for the forests that are gone,
that have been turned into particle board
instead of loam.
We can speak in the courts. In the streets.
We can take action. We can do this.

Notes

#MeToo: Women in Touch with Their Anger

"She has come to love them, the ugly toads, the venomous toads" is paraphrased from Shakespeare's *As You Like It*, Act 2, Scene 1, lines 12–17.

Women and Nature

"I start with the seedling, and I don't want to leave it. I don't feel I really know the story if I don't watch the plant all the way along. So I know every plant in the field" is from *A Feeling For the Organism: The Life and Work of Barbara McClintock*, by Evelyn Fox Keller (Times Books, 1984).

"A forest is a cooperative system" is from an interview with Suzanne Simard by Diane Toomey, *Yale Environment 360*, September, 2016.

The phrase "trees talk" is from Suzanne Simard's TED Talk, *How trees talk to each other*, July, 2016.

". . . I stood, as darkness fell, with one hand on the still warm trunk of a tree and looked at the sparkling of an early moon . . ." is from *In The Shadow of Man*, by Jane Goodall (Mariner Books, 2010). The full quote is: " The beauty was always there, but moments of true awareness were rare. They would come, unannounced; perhaps when I was watching the pale flush preceding dawn; or looking up through the rustling leaves of some giant forest tree into the greens and browns and the black shadows and the occasionally ensured bright fleck of blue sky; or when I stood, as darkness fell, with one hand on the still warm trunk of a tree and looked at the sparkling of an early moon on the never still, softly sighing water of Lake Tanganyika."

The quote "you can't do it alone" is from *The Green Belt Movement: Sharing the Approach and the Experience,* by Wangari Maathai (Lantern Books, 2003). The full quote is: "I'm very conscious of the fact that you can't do it alone. It's teamwork. When you do it alone you run the risk that when you are no longer there nobody else will do it."

At Any Moment, There Could Be a Swerve in a Different Direction

This title echoes a phrase from a June 2016 interview with Craig Childs in *The Sun.*

Rachel Carson

"I moan inside—and I wake in the night and cry out silently for Maine" and "I could never again listen happily to a thrush song if I had not done all I could" are both from *Rachel Carson: Witness for Nature,* by Linda Lear (Mariner Books, 1997).

The phrase "I think of the eagles who came back because of her" refers to the changes that took place after the publication of *Silent Spring* (Houghton Mifflin, 1962). Carson's book led to the passage of the Clean Air Act, the Wilderness Act, the Clean Water Act, and the Endangered Species Act and paved the way for the establishment of the Environmental Protection Agency.

Taking Action

"giant needles": Vermont and Maryland have banned fracking.

The lines "To see soldiers who wear camouflage . . . kneel in front of the Sioux and say they're sorry" refers to the events of December 5, 2016, at Standing Rock, when Wesley Clark Jr., son of NATO Supreme Commander Wesley Clark Sr., apologized to Sioux leader Phyllis Young and Lakota leader Leonard Crow Dog for genocide committed by the U.S. government. A group of veterans joined him, kneeling and asking for forgiveness.

We Have the Power to Pull Back from the Brink

The structure of this poem owes much to "The Voice of Robert Desnos," by Robert Desnos, from *The Selected Poems of Robert Desnos* (Ecco Press, 1991).

The phrase "the ones who have come back" refers to a quote from a December 26, 2017 *U.S. News & World Report* article that "starfish are making a comeback on the West Coast, four years after a mysterious wasting disease killed millions."

The phrase "*a twelve-year-old boy planted a million trees*" refers to Felix Finkbeiner, a German schoolboy who planted trees and launched Plant-for-the-Planet.

Why There Is Reason to Hope

The beginning of the poem echoes lines from "Gentle Now, Don't Add to Heartache" in *Well Then There Now,* by Juliana Spahr (David R. Godine, 2011). Also, "a girl in a raincoat protesting in front of the Swedish Parliament" refers to teenage activist Greta Thunberg and her protests about climate change.

21 Kids Sue the Government for Not Protecting Them from Climate Change

Our Children's Trust is a nonprofit organization suing the federal government for inaction on climate change. The lawsuit is called *Juliana v. United States.*

Acknowledgments

Grateful acknowledgment is made to the editors of the following magazines, blogs, and anthologies where some of these poems first appeared: The Sun; Buddha Weekly; The American Journal of Poetry; Sisyphus; Rise Up Review; Take a Stand: Art Against Hate (Raven Chronicles Press); Kalliope; An Outbreak of Peace (Arachne Press); Vox Populi; America, We Call Your Name: Poems of Resistance and Resilience (Sixteen Rivers Press); and Is It Hot in Here, Or Is It Just Me? (Social Justice Anthologies, Beautiful Cadaver Press). "Lesions" was first published in *Practicing the Truth* (Autumn House Press) and is reprinted with permission.

DESIGN AND PRODUCTION

Text and cover design: Chiquita Babb

Cover painting: "Mill Valley Lumber"
Copyright © 2015 by Tom Killion

Author photograph: Stephanie Mohan

This book was typeset in Adobe Garamond, an old-style serif typeface
named for sixteenth-century Parisian engraver Claude Garamond
(Garamont). The font was created by Robert Slimbach and released in
1989 by Adobe with italics based on the designs of Garamond's assistant,
Robert Granjon.

This book was printed by 1st World Publishing.